This book belongs to:

Anastasia

THE CHARLES HOSMER MORSE MUSEUM OF AMERICAN ART, WINTER PARK, FLORIDA

The Charles Hosmer Morse Museum of American Art houses the world's most comprehensive collection of works by Louis Comfort Tiffany, including jewelry, pottery, paintings, glass, leaded glass, windows, lamps, his chapel interior for the 1893 World's Columbian Exposition in Chicago, and art and architectural objects from his Long Island estate, Laurelton Hall. The museum's holdings also include American art pottery, and late 19th- and early 20th-century American paintings, graphics, and decorative art.

Louis Comfort Tiffany helped to revive the art of stained glass in America. Nature was a great source of artistic inspiration. The panels below are from a large window representing the Four Seasons from Tiffany's award-winning exhibit at the 1900 Exposition Universelle, Paris's world's fair.

Louis Comfort Tiffany (American, 1848–1933), *Four Seasons* window, ca.1899–1900. Leaded glass, various dimensions. The Charles Hosmer Morse Museum of American Art, 57-017–57-019, 62-033

Create your own panel below. What elements from nature would you include to represent your favorite season?

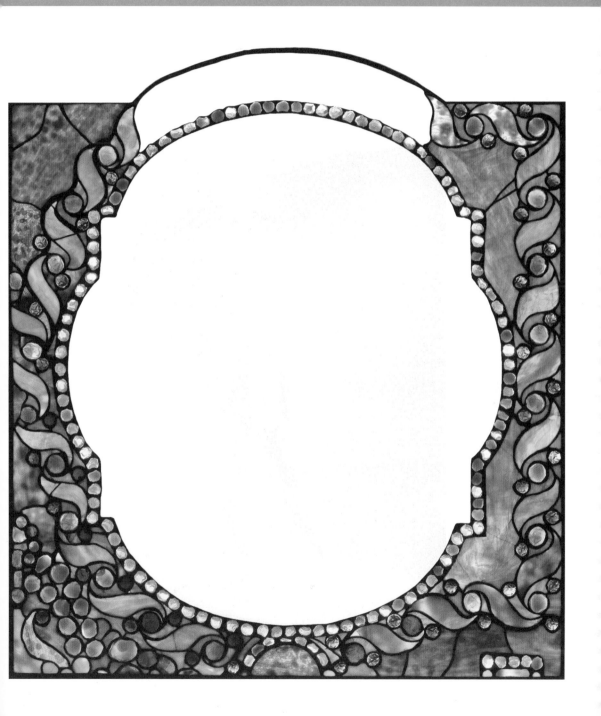

NORTON SIMON MUSEUM, PASADENA, CALIFORNIA

The Norton Simon Museum is known as one of the world's most remarkable private art collections. On view are celebrated works of art from the early Renaissance through the Modern era, and one of the country's finest collections of South and Southeast Asian art.

....

Edgar Degas was a 19th-century French artist, widely known for depicting the subject of dance in his artwork. For the only sculpture that Degas would exhibit during his lifetime, he chose to portray Marie van Goethem, a Belgian teenager who was a ballet student in Paris, standing in this classic pose. The original beeswax sculpture, made around 1880, is now in the National Gallery of Art in Washington; the one you see here, from the Norton Simon Museum, is one of 32 casts that were made after the original. It is made of bronze and dressed with a real tutu. Her ponytail is tied with a splendid satin bow.

Norton Simon Museum

Edgar Degas (French, 1834–1917), *Little Dancer, Aged Fourteen*, 1878–1881, Copper alloy, 37⅝ x 13³/₁₆ x 9¹⁵/₁₆ in. Norton Simon Art Foundation, M.1977.02.70.S

Design a costume for the *Little Dancer* using crayons, collaged paper, or fabric.

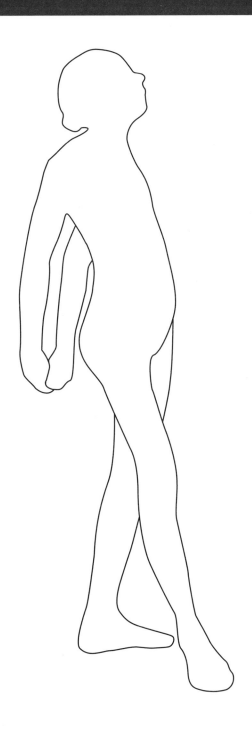

PUTNAM MUSEUM AND SCIENCE CENTER, DAVENPORT, IOWA

The Putnam Museum and Science Center was founded in 1867 as the Davenport Academy of Natural Sciences. Today it houses a giant-screen theater, a hands-on science center focused on S.T.E.M. concepts, and natural history and cultural exhibits. The Putnam Museum is a vibrant destination alive with distinctive multisensory experiences where all generations explore and learn. The museum inspires spirited dialogue and action by acquainting people with the uniqueness of the region, fostering appreciation for our connections to world cultures, and immersing visitors in the wonders of the natural world that surrounds and unites us.

Three thousand years ago, in ancient Egypt, a coffin was created for Isis Neferit, a chantress in the Temple of Isis. She died during Egypt's 21st Dynasty (1070–945 BC). Her name and images of her pouring libations in the afterlife appear on her coffin. The funerary mask on the mummy, donated along with the coffin, helped scholars determine that the mummy inside was in fact not Isis Neferit and was indeed from a different dynasty. The identity of the female mummy acquired with the coffin, and the location of the mummy of Isis Neferit, are still unknown today.

Coffin of Isis Neferit, 21st Dynasty (1070–945 BC), and unidentified funerary mask. Putnam Museum and Science Center

To the ancient Egyptians, names were equally important in life and death. Their belief was that for the soul to be reunited with the body, the name of the deceased needed to be preserved. Names were often found on coffins and sarcophagi, written in hieroglyphs that identified the mummy within. Egyptian hieroglyphs date as far back as 3,300 BC, and there are roughly 500 known symbols. Use the hieroglyphic alphabet to write your name in the cartouche frame below and see how it would have looked in ancient Egyptian.

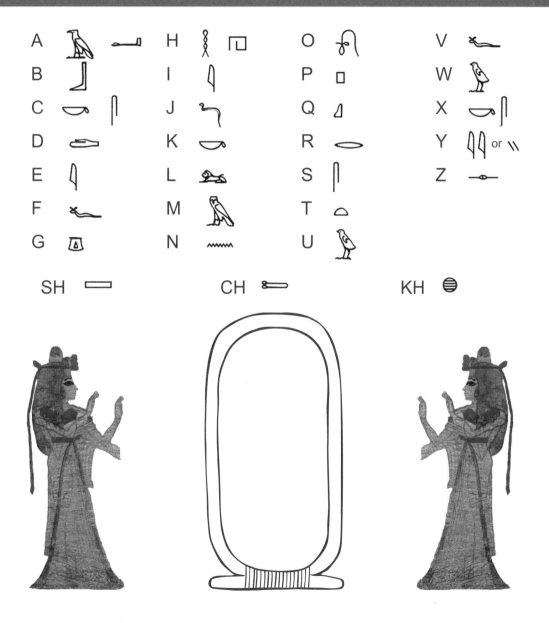

THE NATIONAL WWII MUSEUM, NEW ORLEANS, LOUISIANA

Originally founded in 2000 as the D-Day Museum, The National WWII Museum offers a compelling blend of sweeping narrative and poignant personal detail. The museum features immersive exhibits, multimedia experiences, and an expansive collection of artifacts and first-person oral histories to take visitors inside the story of the war that changed the world: why it was fought, how it was won, and what it means today.

World War II brought not only material and food shortages, but also a lack of manpower in industry. With many able-bodied men joining the armed forces, the government looked to women to fill these labor gaps. Propaganda posters motivated women to work tirelessly while their loved ones were abroad, secure their present and future careers with training, and "do the job he left behind." Through the posters, women were publicly praised for their war work. Women workers in defense industries grew by more than 450 percent during the war.

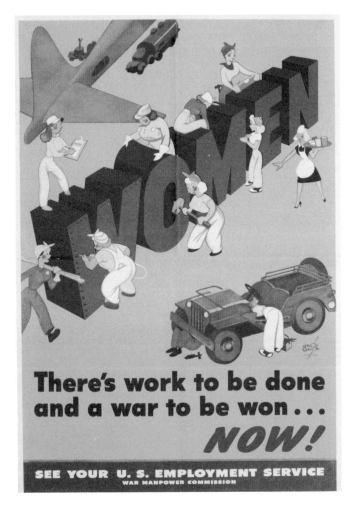

Poster created by the US Employment Service, War Manpower Commission, 1944. National WWII Museum; gift of Anne and Jack Kelsey, 2013.077.119

Draw your own motivational poster.

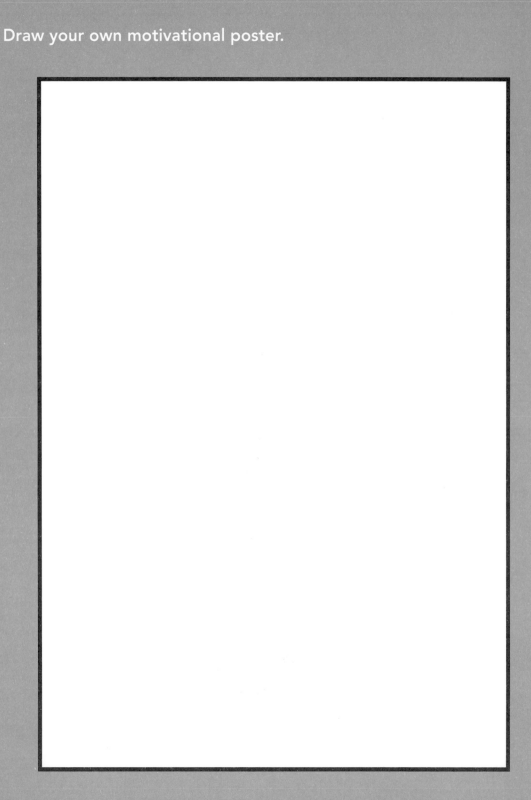

THE BARNES FOUNDATION, PHILADELPHIA AND MERION, PENNSYLVANIA

The Barnes Foundation—including an art collection housed in Philadelphia and an arboretum in Merion—was established in 1922 by Dr. Albert C. Barnes, a Philadelphia native who trained as a physician at the University of Pennsylvania before making a fortune as a pharmaceutical entrepreneur. Barnes's magnificent art collection is particularly famous for its Post-Impressionist and early Modern paintings. They are distinctively displayed in arrangements that incorporate old master paintings, African sculpture, American paintings and decorative arts, antiquities from the Mediterranean region and Asia, and Native American ceramics, jewelry, and textiles. The installations, unchanged since Barnes's death in 1951, were designed by him to show that the formal building blocks of art—light, line, color, and space—are universal and eternal.

....

Like many African peoples, the Yaure of the central Ivory Coast have made masks that are used in special ceremonies. Masks are believed to connect humans and nature, and this particular mask represents a powerful figure known as Yu. The carved lines of the mask define Yu's human and animal features.

THE BARNES FOUNDATION

Face mask, Yaure people,19th–early 20th century. Wood and pigment, 23⅝ x 6½ x 5⁹⁄₁₆ in. The Barnes Foundation, A260

Yu lives in the lines that connect the animal and human shapes that make up the Yaure face mask. Using as many types of lines as you can, sketch your own animal superpower mask.

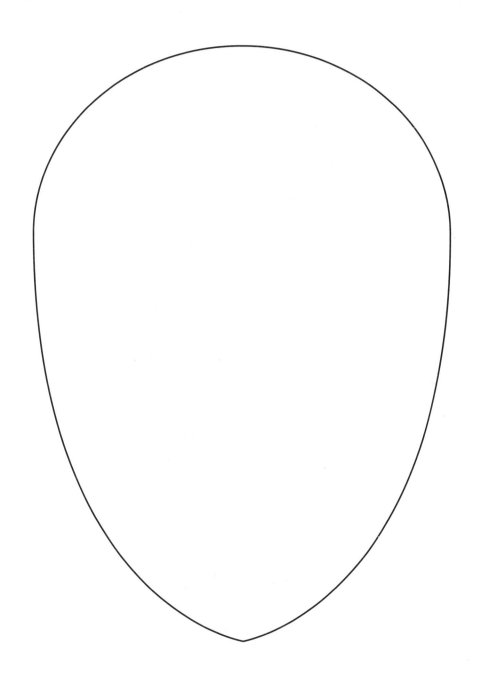

AH-TAH-THI-KI MUSEUM, CLEWISTON, FLORIDA

The Ah-Tah-Thi-Ki Museum was founded to celebrate, preserve, and interpret the culture and history of the Seminole tribe of Florida and does so with a premier collection of Seminole artifacts. It was the first tribally owned museum to be accredited by the American Alliance of Museums.

....

This Seminole beaded cloth shoulder bag, or bandolier bag, was once owned by Osceola, one of the best-known Seminole warriors of the 19th century. Heavily beaded, the bag is constructed from a plain-weave red wool cloth that is backed with printed cotton fabric. It could be worn either across the chest from shoulder to hip, or looped around the back of the neck. The triangle flap protected items carried within the bag.

SEMINOLE TRIBE OF FLORIDA
AH-TAH-THI-KI
M U S E U M
A PLACE TO LEARN. A PLACE TO REMEMBER.

Bandolier, Seminole beaded cloth shoulder bag once owned by Osceola (Billy Powell, Seminole, ca.1804–1838). Wool, cotton, and beads sewn on in a two-thread method. 12¾ x 27⅛ in. Ah-Tah-Thi-Ki Museum, 1997.30.1

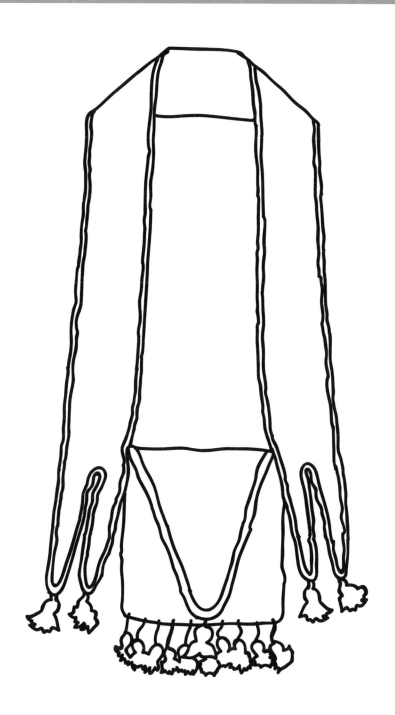

BELL MUSEUM OF NATURAL HISTORY, MINNEAPOLIS, MINNESOTA

The Bell Museum is the state of Minnesota's natural history museum, founded in 1872 and part of the University of Minnesota's College of Food, Agricultural and Natural Resource Sciences. The museum will open a new building and planetarium to better serve its mission to ignite curiosity and wonder, explore our connections to nature and the universe, and create a better future for our evolving world.

....

Natural history museums teach visitors about the science behind the world around them, and they also aim to inspire people to create a better future for our evolving world. Honeybees play a critical role in our ecosystem as pollinators of the food we need to survive. We can help them get the food they need, too, by planting pollinator-friendly plants.

BELL MUSEUM
OF NATURAL HISTORY

UNIVERSITY OF MINNESOTA
Driven to Discover℠

Photograph courtesy of the Bell Museum of Natural History at the University of Minnesota

Honeybees can travel five miles away from their colony to find pollen and nectar. They need lots of energy to get back home! Complete the maze below to help the honeybee get back to the hive.

Solution in back of book.

DE YOUNG MUSEUM, SAN FRANCISCO, CALIFORNIA

The de Young is one of the two museums in the Fine Arts Museums of San Francisco, the city's largest public arts institution. The de Young originated from the 1894 California Midwinter International Exposition and became the city's first art museum, located in the heart of Golden Gate Park. The present copper-clad landmark building, designed by Herzog and de Meuron, opened in October 2005. It showcases the institution's significant collections of American painting, sculpture, and decorative arts from the 17th to the 21st centuries; art from Africa, Oceania, and the Americas; costume and textile arts; and international modern and contemporary art.

....

Chiura Obata created this woodcut of Yosemite Falls, a vast and lush natural feature of Yosemite National Park with waterfalls over 2,400 feet tall! The top of the tree in the front and center of the composition hints that this enormous landscape continues beyond the frame.

de Young

**Fine Arts
Museums of
San Francisco**

Chiura Obata. *Evening Glow of Yosemite Waterfall, Yosemite National Park, California*, from the *World Landscape Series*, 1930. Color woodcut on paper, 15¹¹/₁₆ x 11 in. Fine Arts Museums of San Francisco, 1963.30.3126.23

Use Obata's composition as a starting point to draw the landscape as you imagine it continues around and beyond these falls.

THE WALTERS ART MUSEUM, BALTIMORE, MARYLAND

The Walters Art Museum is internationally renowned for its collection of art, and is one of only a few museums in the world to present a panorama of art from the third millennium BC to the early 20th century. The collection was amassed largely by two men, William and Henry Walters, and eventually handed over to the City of Baltimore.

....

This egg was created in 1901 by the jeweler Fabergé as a present for Marie Feodorovna, the dowager empress of Russia. Fabergé decorated its eggs with precious materials and always hid a surprise. Inside this one is a miniature version of Marie's palace.

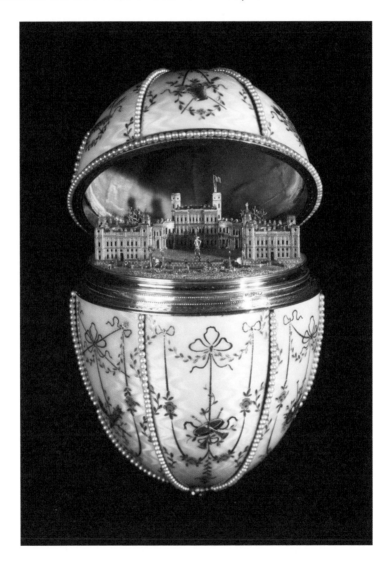

House of Fabergé, *Gatchina Palace Egg*, 1901. Gold, en plein enamel, silver gilding, portrait diamonds, rock crystal, and seed pearls, 5 x 3⁹⁄₁₆ in. Walters Art Museum; Acquired by Henry Walters, 1930, 44.500

Design your own Fabergé egg. How will you decorate it?
What surprise will you hide inside?

THE DALÍ MUSEUM, ST. PETERSBURG, FLORIDA

There has never been a place like the Dalí Museum. This magnificent building, located on the waterfront in the heart of beautiful downtown St. Petersburg, is home to an unparalleled collection of renowned artist Salvador Dalí's finest works—filled with his iconic melting clocks, imaginative visual illusions, and avant-garde symbols. The Dalí Museum features more than 2,000 works by Dalí, including oil paintings, watercolors, drawings, prints, photographs, sculptures, and objets d'art. It is the largest collection of the artist's work outside of Spain, and one of the most acclaimed collections in the world of art by a single modern artist.

....

Dalí painted this very early self-portrait when he was only 14 years old. The artist is shown painting at his easel framed in a open doorway showing the pink morning sky.

Salvador Dalí (Spanish, 1904–1989), *Self-Portrait*, 1918–1919. Oil on canvas, 10½ x 8¼ in. The Dalí Museum; Gift of A. Reynolds & Eleanor Morse, 1980.5. Worldwide rights © Salvador Dalí. Fundacion Gala-Salvador Dalí, (Artists Rights Society), 2016/ In the USA © Salvador Dalí Museum, Inc. St. Petersburg, FL 2016.

Dalí used pinks and blues to capture the morning light in his studio. Try changing these colors to create an evening effect.

ADDISON GALLERY OF AMERICAN ART, ANDOVER, MASSACHUSETTS

Located on the campus of Phillips Academy, the Addison Gallery's collection of American art is one of the most comprehensive in the world, including more than 17,000 objects spanning the 18th century to the present. In a typical year, the Addison presents approximately twelve shows, including both permanent collection installations and major traveling exhibitions, carefully balanced to represent a wide range of art, across time and media. The Addison is committed to serving the public through free admission and all education programs are offered at no charge.

. . . .

This portrait painted by Thomas Eakins features the American scientist Professor Henry A. Rowland in his work environment. Eakins also constructed an elaborate gilded chestnut frame for the canvas into which he carved scientific symbols and notations from Rowland's notebooks.

Thomas Eakins (American, 1844–1916), *Professor Henry A. Rowland*, 1897. Oil on canvas, 80¼ x 54 in. Addison Gallery of American Art, Phillips Academy; gift of Stephen C. Clark, Esq., 1931.5

Draw a portrait of yourself or someone you know. How might you design a frame that represents this person?

SCIENCE CENTER OF IOWA, DES MOINES, IOWA

The Science Center of Iowa (SCI) engages and inspires visitors by bringing learning to life. Centrally located in downtown Des Moines, SCI's hands-on exhibits, special-format theaters and unique programming attract Iowans and distant visitors alike.

....

Standing at 15 feet tall, the Ball Wall is a series of tubes, fans, connectors, levers, and pulleys that move a ball from one point to another. By controlling certain points along the wall and using air pressure—applying Bernoulli's principle that pressure is reduced when the speed of flow is increased—balls can be moved from one component of the wall to the next!

Connect the tubes to create your own path on the Ball Wall. Can you make a path that can move a ball through the entire Ball Wall?

MCNAY ART MUSEUM, SAN ANTONIO, TEXAS

Built by artist and collector Marion Koogler McNay in the 1920s, her Spanish Colonial residence, the McNay Art Museum, opened in 1954 as the first museum of modern art in Texas. McNay's collection reflected her interest in French painting and Post-Impressionism. Since the museum's founding, the collection has increased in both size and range to include more than 20,000 objects. Modern masters represented in the collection include Paul Gauguin, Vincent van Gogh, Edward Hopper, Georgia O'Keeffe, Henri Matisse, Pablo Picasso, Jackson Pollock, and Pierre-Auguste Renoir.

....

Characteristics of Impressionist paintings include hazy colors, short brush strokes, and outdoor settings. Camille Pissarro often painted in a more realistic style; as he got older, he tried out new Impressionist techniques popular among much younger artists.

theMcNay
McNay Art Museum

Camille Pissarro, *Haymakers Resting*, 1891. Oil on canvas, 25¾ x 32 in. McNay Art Museum; Bequest of Marion Koogler McNay

Imagine a conversation these women might be having.
Fill in the speech bubbles below.

PHOENIX ART MUSEUM, PHOENIX, ARIZONA

An institution of exciting art and learning since 1959, Phoenix Art Museum has become the largest art museum in the southwestern United States, providing access to art from all over the world to the people of Arizona. Throughout the year the museum presents festivals, live performances, and independent art films, plus educational programs for families and schools that enlighten, entertain, and stimulate.

....

The Thorne Miniature Rooms were conceived, designed, and created by Narcissa Niblack Thorne beginning in the 1930s. The rooms faithfully depict architecture and interior design from the 16th century to 1925 in Europe and the United States. Thorne created the rooms, including the one seen below, to house her collection of miniature furniture and accessories she amassed during her world travels. The detailed rooms are built on a scale of 1:12 (1 inch represents 12 inches, or 1 foot).

Phoenix Art Museum

Narcissa Niblack Thorne (American, 1882-1966), *Eighteenth-Century French Drawing Room*, 1932–1937. Mixed media. Phoenix Art Museum; Gift of Niblack Thorne, 1962.79.7

Imagine what your own miniature room might look like. Would it be modern or old-fashioned? One-point-perspective drawings orient objects toward a single vanishing point (the small dot in the center), so your sketch can appear 3-D on a flat page.

Complete the one-point-perspective drawing of the miniature room below. Follow the angles of the lines as you decorate!

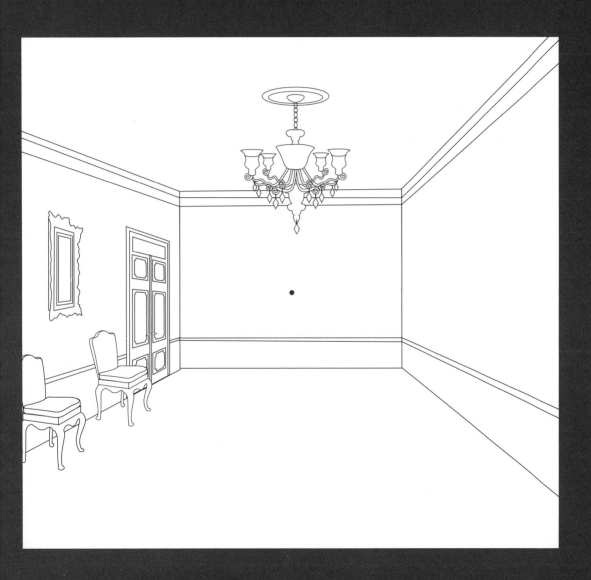

SAINT LOUIS ART MUSEUM, ST. LOUIS, MISSOURI

The Saint Louis Art Museum, located in the Midwest, has a collection of more than 33,000 original works of art, including paintings, sculptures, photographs, and ceramics from a period of time covering more than 5,000 years. The museum is known throughout the world for its collection of American, German, and Chinese art.

Missouri-born artist Nick Cave creates what he calls "soundsuits," or wearable sculptures made of found and recycled materials. He uses old toys, buttons, and fabrics, and considers the sounds these materials will make when the suit is worn. The artist also choreographs dance performances in which the sculptures are brought to life through the dancers' acrobatic movements.

SAINT LOUIS
ART MUSEUM

Nick Cave (American, b. 1959), *Soundsuit*, 2014. Mixed media, including vintage toys, noisemakers, metal, hot pads, fabric, and mannequin, 110 x 60 x 40 in. Saint Louis Art Museum; Funds given by Gary C. Werths and Richard Frimel, 3:2015a–d

Design your own soundsuit. What would you attach to it? Make a list of the materials you would use and the sounds they would make, then draw them on the figure below.

Materials & Sounds:

....

....

....

....

....

....

....

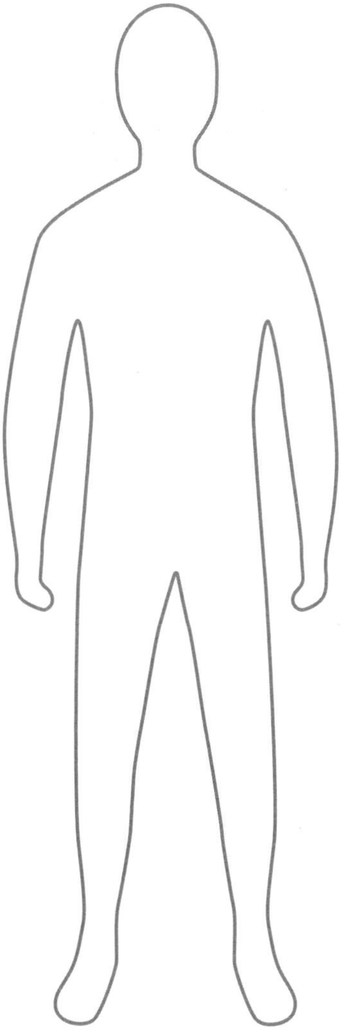

HISTORIC DEERFIELD, DEERFIELD, MASSACHUSSETTS

Historic Deerfield, founded in 1952, is an outdoor museum that focuses on the history and culture of the Connecticut River Valley and early New England. It has a dual mission of educating the public about the lifestyles of the diverse people who lived in the village of Deerfield long ago, and of preserving antique buildings and collections of regional furniture, silver, textiles, and other decorative arts. The museum gives tours of 12 historic houses built in the 18th and 19th centuries, and has a modern exhibition space where visitors can explore its collections.

Pole stands with embroidered screens, such as the one below, were designed to shield the face from the hot fireplace as well as to boast the accomplishments of a daughter who had learned her lessons at school. Miss Sarah Leavitt of Greenfield, Massachusetts, embroidered the screen of this stand in 1810.

 Historic Deerfield
Opening Doorways To The Past.

Pole screen with embroidery by Sarah Leavitt (American, 1797–1837) and stand by Daniel Clay (American, 1770–1848), Greenfield, Massachusetts, 1810. Wrapped metallic silk thread, plain weave, cream silk, sequins, watercolors, and cherry. Historic Deerfield; Museum Collections Fund, HD 2007.19. © Historic Deerfield.

POLK MUSEUM OF ART, LAKELAND, FLORIDA

Named one of the top ten art museums in Florida and an affiliate of the Smithsonian Institution, the Polk Museum of Art is a private, non-profit and nationally accredited art museum. The museum has nurtured one of Florida's most impressive and diverse collections of fine and decorative arts from around the world. Currently, the permanent collection at the Polk Museum of Art features an extensive collection of contemporary and modern art, as well as an array of Pre-Columbian, Asian, European, and American decorative arts.

....

Tsukioka Yoshitoshi is widely recognized as the last great master of *ukiyo-e*, a style of Japanese woodblock print. He used his artwork to ensure the preservation of Japan's cultural heritage. The woman in this image is wearing a kimono, a traditional Japanese garment.

Tsukioka Yoshitoshi (Japanese, 1839-1892), *Disagreeable, The Appearance of a Young Lady from Nagoya During the Ansei Era*, 1888. Woodblock print, 14¼ x 9½ in. Polk Museum of Art; Gift of Robert Meyer, 1995.39.23

WADSWORTH ATHENEUM MUSEUM OF ART, HARTFORD, CONNECTICUT

Founded in 1842 by Hartford arts patron Daniel Wadsworth, the Wadsworth Atheneum Museum of Art is the oldest continuously operating public art museum in the United States. The museum's nearly 50,000 works of art span 5,000 years, from Greek and Roman antiquities to the first museum collection of American contemporary art. The Wadsworth Atheneum has paved the way for encyclopedic museums across the country; it was the first museum in America to purchase works by Caravaggio, Frederic Church, Joseph Cornell, Salvador Dalí, and Joan Miró, and was the first in the country to exhibit major surveys of works by Italian Baroque masters, Surrealists, and Pablo Picasso.

....

This painting depicts the arrest of King Louis XVI of France. At the center is the king saying a tearful goodbye to his family while the guards at the left wait to take him away. The artist has given each figure an individual emotional reaction, from the angry grimace of the soldiers to the anguished disbelief of Marie-Antoinette, who throws her hands in the air. The king's arrest was an important moment in the French Revolution, marking the abolition of the French monarchy.

WADSWORTH ATHENEUM
MUSEUM OF ART

Mather Brown (American, active England, 1761–1831), *Louis XVI Saying Farewell to His Family*, 1793. Oil on canvas, 86 x 111 in. Wadsworth Atheneum Museum of Art; The Ella Gallup Sumner and Mary Catlin Sumner Collection Fund, 1980.2

The artist has included so many details in this painting! Each one helps tell the story of this moment in history. Look closely to take in the entire work, and then pick a single detail that jumps out at you. Now draw it in the circle below:

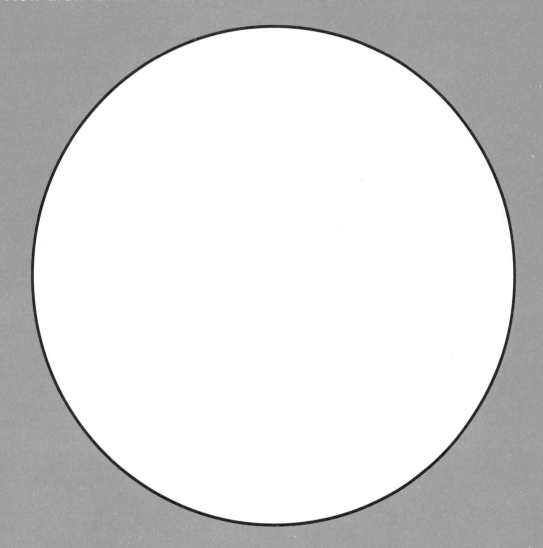

Did you notice anything new about the painting after drawing your detail? Why do you think the artist included it? What do you think your detail adds to the work as a whole?

LEGION OF HONOR, SAN FRANCISCO CALIFORNIA

The Legion of Honor is one of the two museums in the Fine Arts Museums of San Francisco, the city's largest public arts institution. The Legion of Honor building and collections were inspired by the French pavilion at San Francisco's Panama-Pacific International Exposition of 1915, which was itself a replica of the Palais de la Légion d'Honneur in Paris. The museum opened in 1924 on a bluff in Lincoln Park, overlooking the Golden Gate Bridge, and was originally dedicated to French art. Today its holdings span 4,000 years and include European painting, sculpture, and decorative arts; ancient art from the Mediterranean basin; and the largest collection of works on paper in the American West.

Before the advent of photography, portraits were created by painters. Massimo Stanzione, a Baroque painter from Naples, created a sense of magnificence and splendor through his use of detail in this woman's clothing. She holds a rooster, which serves as a symbol to give us ideas about her and her life.

Legion of Honor

Fine Arts
Museums of
San Francisco

Massimo Stanzione. *Woman in Neapolitan Costume*, ca. 1635. Oil on canvas, 46¾ x 38¼ in.
Fine Arts Museums of San Francisco, 1997.32

If you were to sit for a painted portrait, what would you wear? What would you hold to help us understand you?

NATIONAL BUILDING MUSEUM, WASHINGTON, DC

The National Building Museum is dedicated to architecture, engineering, and design. It tells stories about what buildings are, what they do, and how they are designed. The museum has a collection of work by sculptor and architect Raymond Kaskey, who designs public art for buildings and memorials, helping to create places where people go to learn about and remember historical events.

....

This panel is from Raymond Kaskey's plans for the National World War II Memorial in Washington, DC. It shows women soldiers loading their belongings as they get ready to go to the war front.

Raymond Kaskey, model for World War II Memorial, Atlantic Panel 3, Women in Military, full scale. National Building Museum; Kaskey Studio

What event do you want people to remember?
Draw your own scene here.

CUMMER MUSEUM OF ART AND GARDENS, JACKSONVILLE, FLORIDA

The Cummer Museum of Art and Gardens is the largest fine arts museum in Northeast Florida. In 1958, art collector, garden enthusiast, and civic leader Ninah M. H. Cummer bequeathed the art collection and riverfront home she shared with her husband, Arthur, to create the museum. Today, the core collection of 60 pieces from the Cummers' estate has grown to include nearly 5,000 works of art. The 2.5 acres of historic gardens, set against the backdrop of the St. Johns River, serve as a centerpiece of beauty for all to enjoy.

....

Edmund Greacen probably painted this view of the Brooklyn Bridge from the window of his apartment building on East 18th Street in New York City. Through broken brushwork and sketchy atmospheric color, the artist portrays the twin lives of the city, the industrial city in the foreground and the serene Brooklyn skyline and the East River in the background.

Edmund William Greacen (American, 1877–1949), *Brooklyn Bridge, East River*, 1916. Oil on canvas, 37 x 37½ in. Cummer Museum of Art and Gardens; Gift of Mr. and Mrs. Rene Faure (Daughter of Edmond Greacen, Nan Greacen Faure), AG.1972.2.1

Examine Greacen's cityscape painting. What do you see in the foreground, middle ground, and background?

Imagine that you're in the painting. What would you hear, see, and smell? Draw your own cityscape below, or create one using colored construction paper or newspaper.

NEW-YORK HISTORICAL SOCIETY, NEW YORK, NEW YORK

The New-York Historical Society, founded in 1804, is one of America's pre-eminent cultural institutions, dedicated to fostering research, presenting history and art exhibitions, and hosting public programs that reveal the dynamism of history and its influence on the world today. The New-York Historical is the oldest museum in New York City and has a mission to explore the richly layered political, cultural and social history of the city, the state of New York, and the nation, as well as serving as a national forum for the discussion of issues surrounding the making and meaning of history.

New York City was the nation's first capital and the site of the first presidential inauguration. Keith Shaw Williams's painting recreates the ceremony as George Washington places his hand on the Bible and takes the first presidential oath of office on the balcony of Federal Hall in lower Manhattan:

> *I do solemnly swear that I will faithfully execute the Office of President of the United States, and will to the best of my ability, preserve, protect and defend the Constitution of the United States.*

NEW-YORK
HISTORICAL
SOCIETY
MUSEUM & LIBRARY
MAKING HISTORY MATTER

Keith Shaw Williams, (American, 1906–1951). *Inauguration of George Washington at Federal Hall, New York City*, 1789. Oil on canvas, 83 x 72 in. New-York Historical Society, 1938.403

An oath is a solemn or important promise, spoken out loud for other people to hear and bear witness. They are used in many situations when a person needs to be true to what they say.

Can you list other examples or situations where a person might be asked to take an oath today?

1. ....

2. ....

3. ....

HIGH MUSEUM OF ART, ATLANTA, GEORGIA

The High Museum of Art is a leading art museum in the southeastern United States. With more than 15,000 artworks in its permanent collection, the High has an extensive anthology of 19th- and 20th-century American art and decorative arts, significant holdings of European paintings, a growing collection of African American art, and burgeoning collections of modern and contemporary art, photography, folk and self-taught art, and African art. The High is also dedicated to supporting and collecting works by Southern artists.

Nellie Mae Rowe's passion to create was inspired by everyday events, friends and family, memories, and a persistent desire to celebrate. Rowe decorated her home in Georgia, which she fondly referred to as Nellie's Playhouse, with brilliantly colored drawings like *Happy Days*, below.

HIGH MUSEUM OF ART ATLANTA

Nellie Mae Rowe (American, 1900–1982), *Happy Days*, 1981. Crayon and graphite on paper. 18 x 24 in. High Museum of Art, Atlanta T. Marshall Hahn Collection, 1997.105

Fill this page with drawings of the people, animals, and things that make you happy!

GEORGIA O'KEEFFE MUSEUM, SANTA FE, NEW MEXICO

The Georgia O'Keeffe Museum opened to the public in July 1997. One of the most significant artists of the 20th century, Georgia O'Keeffe was devoted to creating imagery that expressed what she called "the wideness and wonder of the world as I live in it." O'Keeffe's images—instantly recognizable as her own—include abstractions; large-scale depictions of flowers, leaves, rocks, shells, bones and other natural forms; New York cityscapes; and paintings of the unusual shapes and colors of architectural and landscape forms of northern New Mexico.

....

Georgia O'Keeffe was inspired by the beauty of the New Mexico desert. From her bedroom window in Abiquiu, she could see the vast sky above, hills and trees below, and a road stretching into the distance. She enjoyed this view so much that she completed several paintings of the mesa and the road to the east.

Georgia O'Keeffe Museum

Top: View from O'Keeffe's bedroom looking north, 2007. Photograph by Herbert Lotz, © Georgia O'Keeffe Museum. Bottom: Georgia O'Keeffe (American, 1887–1986), *Mesa and Road East*, 1952. Oil on canvas, 26 x 36 in. Georgia O'Keeffe Museum. Gift of The Georgia O'Keeffe Foundation (2006.05.234) © Georgia O'Keeffe Museum

Familiar places can be great as sources for artistic inspiration! What do you see when you look outside your window?

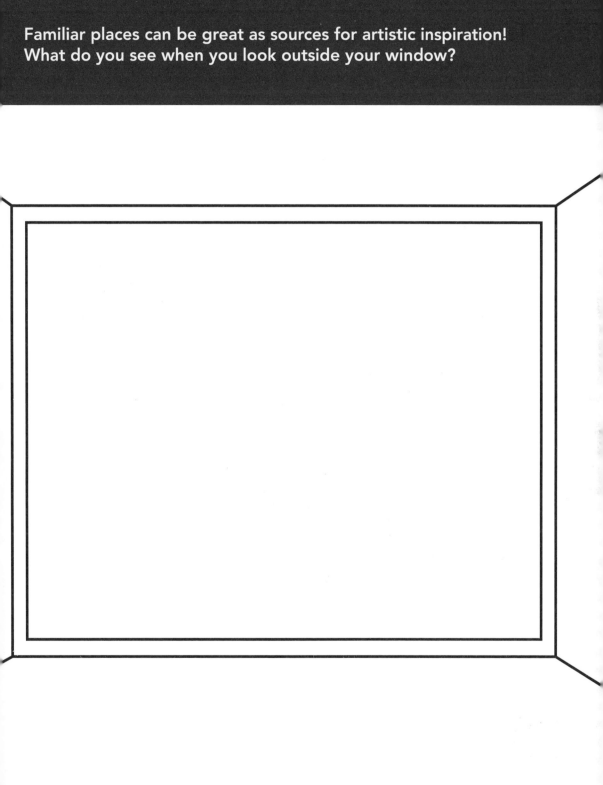

DENNOS MUSEUM CENTER, TRAVERSE CITY, MICHIGAN

The Dennos Museum Center at Northwestern Michigan College is northwest Lower Michigan's premier cultural center, offering programming in the visual and performing arts and sciences since 1991. The museum's collection of Inuit art of the Canadian Arctic is one of the largest in the United States, with more than 1,500 objects. In addition, the Dennos exhibits and collects works by artists from the region and beyond, with a recent international focus on artists from East Asia.

This raven is shown holding an ulu, a traditional tool used by Inuit women. The raven is an important creature in Inuit storytelling tradition, associated with the creation of the Earth and often depicted as a powerful shape-shifter and trickster.

Ningeokuluk Teevee (Cape Dorset, Nunavut Territory, Canada, b. 1963), *Raven with Ulu*, 2014. Stonecut and stencil on Gampi Torinoko paper 24/50, 20½ x 25 in. Printed by Ashoona Ashoona (Cape Dorset, Nunavut Territory, Canada, b. 1974). Reproduced with the permission of Dorset Fine Arts. Dennos Museum Center; Museum purchase, FY 2014/15, 2014.010.001

Create your own intricate patterns to decorate this raven. Will you use different colors or just one? Can you include an ulu as part of the pattern?

WYCLIFFE DISCOVERY CENTER, ORLANDO, FLORIDA

The Wycliffe Discovery Center is an interactive experience for people of all ages. Learn about people, languages, and cultures from all over the world and come face to face with groups of people who are waiting for the Bible in their own languages. Hear amazing stories of lives that are being changed as God's Word is translated for others around the world, and find out how you can be a part of it.

Wycliffe is dedicated to helping people translate the Bible into their own language. At the Wycliffe Discovery Center, see people from around the world dressed in their traditional clothing. Learn about different languages and cultures while examining these beautifully designed traditional garments.

Design these traditional outfits with fun colors and designs.
What would you want to wear?

CARNEGIE MUSEUM OF NATURAL HISTORY, PITTSBURGH, PENNSYLVANIA

The Carnegie Museum of Natural History, one of the four Carnegie Museums of Pittsburgh, is among the top six natural history museums in the country. The museum is an active research institution with more than 22 million objects, including a large collection of dinosaurs, gems and minerals, dioramas, and artifacts from ancient Egyptian and Native American cultures.

....

Diplodocus carnegii is the most famous dinosaur in the Carnegie Museum of Natural History's collection of prehistoric fossils. A statue of *Diplodocus carnegii*, nicknamed Dippy, stands in the gardens outside of the museum and wears a variety of scarves to support different events, communities, and causes.

CARNEGIE MUSEUM OF NATURAL HISTORY

Activity illustration by Erin Foster

Dippy loves wearing scarves! Draw Dippy a scarf, hat, or other accessory that the dinosaur will love.

THE DOSEUM, SAN ANTONIO, TEXAS

The DoSeum (The-Doo-See-Um) is San Antonio's only museum just for children where kids learn by doing, creating, and tinkering—instead of just looking and listening. Through joyful learning and discovery, The DoSeum grows minds, connects families, and transforms communities. It also serves as a premier educational resource through developing innovative thinkers capable of meeting the challenges of the 21st century.

....

The Big Climb is 39,000 square feet of interactive outdoor space zoned by age, activity, and noise level. The area features a reimagined bubble area and a 30-foot-high German climbing structure.

Treehouse. Photograph courtesy of The DoSeum

RAILROADERS MEMORIAL MUSEUM, ALTOONA, PENNSYLVANIA

The Railroaders Memorial Museum commemorates the significant contributions of railroad workers and their families to American life and industry. The museum has three full floors of exhibits of Pennsylvania Railroad (PRR) history and Altoona history, a movie theater that shows two short films, and a newly built roundhouse which houses some of their rolling stock.

K4 steam locomotive #1361 was built in Altoona in May 1918 and was retired from service in 1956. It is one of 425 locomotives of that class that saw service before the end of PRR steam locomotive service in 1957. The K4 #1361 is currently under restoration at the Railroaders Memorial Museum.

Color the K4. What number would you assign to the front plate?

NATIONAL COWGIRL MUSEUM AND HALL OF FAME, FORT WORTH, TEXAS

The National Cowgirl Museum and Hall of Fame is the only museum in the world dedicated to honoring the women of the American West who have displayed extraordinary courage and pioneer spirit in their trailblazing efforts. Currently, the museum's archives house more than 4,000 artifacts and information about more than 750 remarkable women. The National Cowgirl Hall of Fame honorees include pioneers, artists, writers, entertainers, humanitarians, business women, educators, ranchers, and rodeo cowgirls. Among them are Sacagawea, principal guide for the Lewis and Clark expedition; painter Georgia O'Keeffe; potter Maria Martinez; writer Laura Ingalls Wilder; sharpshooter Annie Oakley; architect Mary Jane Colter; Enid Justin, who created the multimillion-dollar Nocona Boot Company; Hollywood icon Dale Evans; and U.S Supreme Court Justice Sandra Day O'Connor.

....

During her rodeo career, Tad Lucas competed in relay racing, bronc riding, and trick riding, winning virtually every significant prize available to cowgirls. She was the All-Around Champion and Trick Riding Champion at Madison Square Garden for eight consecutive years. In 1948, Lucas became a charter member of the Girls Rodeo Association, the predecessor of the Women's Professional Rodeo Association. Dubbed the "First Lady of Rodeo," Lucas retired in 1958, leaving behind a winning legacy as a fearless and innovative trick rider that many consider the greatest in rodeo cowgirl history.

Suede jacket worn by Tad Lucas (1902–1990), ca. 1920. National Cowgirl Museum and Hall of Fame

Fringe was originally functional in clothing—pull off a string in case you needed to tie off something, or swat off flies. In Wild West shows and rodeos, fringe was used decoratively to enhance the movement of the riders so they could be easily seen from a distance. Imagine you were performing trick riding in a rodeo. What would your show jacket look like when you are performing?

DENVER ART MUSEUM, DENVER, COLORADO

The Denver Art Museum is an educational, nonprofit resource that sparks creative thinking and expression through transformative experiences with art. Its holdings reflect the city and region, and provide invaluable ways for the community to learn about cultures from around the world. The mission of the Denver Art Museum is to enrich the lives of present and future generations through the acquisition, presentation, and preservation of works of art, supported by exemplary scholarship and public programs related to both its permanent collections and to temporary exhibitions presented by the museum.

....

Frank Mechau grew up in Glenwood Springs, Colorado. He worked for the railroad and as a cattle hand. Mechau felt that the West held the best possible subject matter for his art. "Sports, mountains, canyons, and the history of the West, of which Colorado has more than her share, are subjects from which I hope to fashion [my art]," he said. This painting has a Colorado setting, with mountains along the horizon. Mechau was also inspired by the energy and beauty of horses, a common source of dynamic form and movement in his paintings.

Frank Mechau (American, 1904–1946), *Rodeo-Pickup Man*, 1925–1935. Oil on canvas, 31¾ x 39¼ in. Denver Art Museum; Gift of Anne Evans, 1935.9

Rodeo is a competitive sport that is based on the working practices of and the skills required by cattle ranching. Rodeo events involve horses and other livestock, and are designed to test the skill and speed of the competitors. Competition events include team roping, steer wrestling, bronc riding, bull riding and barrel racing. Young cowboys and cowgirls can participate in rodeo events such as mutton busting and lamb wrangling.

What do you imagine the cowboys in the painting are saying to the horses? For example: "Giddy up!", "Whoa!", or "Easy now!"

....

....

....

How many legs can you see in the painting? ....

How many horses do you see? ....   How many cowboys? ....

Solution (pg 15):

The Museum Store Association (MSA) is a 501(c)3 international organization based in Philadelphia, PA with the mission of advancing the nonprofit retail industry and the success of the professionals engaged in it. With over 1,300 members and eight regional chapters, MSA members and their stores offer products and services that encourage high standards of knowledge and professionalism while representing their institutions to the public.

MUSEUM STORE ASSOCIATION

www.museumstoreassociation.org

70 West 36th Street, New York, NY 10018
161-165 Farringdon Road, London, EC1R 3AL

f ☐ @mudpuppykids
Design © Mudpuppy
www.mudpuppy.com

02/2017 M120216A
Designed in the U.S.A.
Printed in Dongguan, China

ISBN: 978-0-7353-5218-6

9 780735 352186